199861

Lindsey, Frances

Bits and Pieces
and The Smugglers

J

Bits and Pieces
and the Smugglers

Bits and Pieces
and the Smugglers

Frances Lindsay

ILLUSTRATED BY TERRY BURTON

HODDER AND STOUGHTON

LONDON SYDNEY AUCKLAND TORONTO

Also by Frances Lindsay

Mr Bits and Pieces
Bits and Pieces Solves a Mystery

British Library Cataloguing in Publication Data

Lindsay, Frances
   Bits and Pieces and the smugglers. – (Leapfrog)
   I. Title   II. Series
   823'.914[J]   PZ7

ISBN 0-340-35146-2

First published 1984

Published by Hodder and Stoughton Children's Books,
a division of Hodder and Stoughton Ltd,
Mill Road, Dunton Green, Sevenoaks, Kent TN13 2YJ

Printed and bound in Great Britain by
St Edmundsbury Press, Bury St Edmunds, Suffolk

Photoset by Rowland Phototypesetting Ltd,
Bury St Edmunds, Suffolk

Preface

I am indebted to Allen White, Historian, whose book *18th Century Smuggling in Christchurch* prompted me to write this story.

In the Domesday Book the original name for Christchurch appears as Tuinam or Thuinam, later appearing as Twynham. After the rebuilding of the Saxon Church in the Norman Period when the High Altar of the Choir (the monk's church) was dedicated to Christ, Twynham became known as Christchurch. It is twinned with Christchurch, South Island, New Zealand.

One   Cockleshell Cottage

Bits and Pieces the junk man opened the
squeaky gate, crossed the tiny garden to an
iron banded front door, and thrust a large key
in the lock. 'You'd better open it, Mrs G.,' he
said.

'Never mind about that. Let's get inside,'
Mrs Goodheart answered.

Bits and Pieces unlocked the door which
opened into a dark, stuffy room. What little
light there was came from small paned
windows obscured by dirt and dead plants but
as his eyes became accustomed to the gloom he
saw they were in a small, comfortably
furnished room overlooking a tiny paved
courtyard.

'Well, what do you think of it, Mrs G?'
Mrs Goodheart put down the bag she was

carrying and looked around. 'It's nice, very nice and much as I had imagined tho' it's many years since I was here. Poor cousin Edith . . .' She wiped away a tear and Bits and Pieces said gently, 'No tears now. Come and see the rest of your inheritance.'

A door in the kitchen revealed a narrow staircase leading up to two small bedrooms and a minute bathroom and, tears forgotten, Mrs Goodheart immediately started opening windows and checking for signs of damp. Bits and Pieces looked at the deep silled windows. 'They knew how to build in those days. These walls are really thick. Do you know how old the cottage is?'

'Over two hundred years I believe and it's been in Edith's family for most of that time. Now, while I unpack the food you fetch the cases and take those dead plants away. You might rub a cloth over the windows while you're at it.'

Bits and Pieces grinned. 'Which shall I do first, madam?'

'Clean the windows, Cheeky,' Mrs Goodheart retorted.

No sooner was the dirt off the windows than the room was full of sunlight. Mrs Goodheart exclaimed with delight as she carried in a tray of food. 'The more I see of this place the more I like it. Edith was kind to leave it to me.'

'She couldn't have left it to anyone nicer unless it was me,' Bits and Pieces said jocularly, fearing a fresh outbreak of tears.

'Your turn will come,' said Mrs Goodheart. 'Now take those cases upstairs while I find some knives and forks.'

Bits and Pieces was eager to be alone for a few minutes. Unknown to anyone he had a secret, a magic mop hidden inside his jacket, and a muffled whisper had told him it had come to life.

The junk man had been given the mop by a kind witch named Artemisia who had promised it would be a good friend to him. Her words had come true. Whenever Bits and Pieces needed advice or was in trouble – usually because he had done something silly – Moppy would come to his aid.

He pulled the mop from his pocket. 'What is it?' he whispered.

'Artemisia says . . .'

'Bring down my woolly with you; it's in the front bedroom,' Mrs Goodheart called.

'I will.' Bits and Pieces held the mop closer. 'What did you say, Moppy?'

'Artemisia . . .'

'And see if my glasses are on the chest,' Mrs Goodheart went on.

'All right.'

But a third attempt to talk to Moppy ended in failure. The mop refused to say a word, and putting it back in his pocket, Bits and Pieces collected Mrs Goodheart's woolly and glasses and went downstairs.

She handed him a large slice of homemade meat pie. 'Eat up. It's all you'll get until I've had a chance to look at that cooker.'

Bits and Pieces was too excited to eat. All he could think about was Artemisia. It was infuriating that Mrs Goodheart had interrupted just as Moppy was going to tell him something about the witch. Was it a message perhaps, an instruction for Bits and Pieces to go somewhere, do something? And if Moppy continued to sulk how could he find out?

As if reading his thoughts the mop dug him in his ribs and Bits and Pieces cried aloud. Mrs Goodheart looked up. 'What's up? Got cramp?'

'Sort of.'

'You ought to stretch your legs after eating all that pie. Why, you've hardly touched it.

What's the matter? Didn't you like it? Are you feeling ill?' A look of consternation made Bits and Pieces say hurriedly, 'It was fine, Mrs G. I'm just not hungry. Too excited about coming away.'

'Then off you go and have a nice walk. Get an appetite for supper while I have forty winks.'

As soon as he was on his own, Bits and Pieces tried again to talk to the mop but without success and, disappointed, he set off on his walk.

The winter had been hard, with weeks of frost and snow making work difficult for Jim who earned a living tramping the streets collecting bits and pieces of junk which he sold at the Saturday market. People out of work could ill-afford to give away things and Bits and Pieces, as Jim had become known, found it increasingly hard to earn enough money to keep himself.

Then, soon after Easter, his neighbour, Mrs Goodheart, learnt that a distant cousin had died, leaving her cottage to Mrs Goodheart. She was both elated and worried. What could she do with a cottage so far from home? What sort of condition was it in? She was sure she would never want to live in it but would she be able to sell it?

'There's only one way to find out. You must go and see for yourself,' Bits and Pieces had told her.

'I haven't been away from home for over twenty years.'

'Then it's time you went!'

A gleam had come into Mrs Goodheart's eye. 'I'll go if you'll come with me. I couldn't possibly go by myself.'

It was easy to promise he would, for he was sure she would never leave her home but less than two weeks later they were here in Twynham and, unknown to Bits and Pieces, he was on the threshold of another exciting adventure.

As he wandered through the narrow streets he thought how lucky he was to be away on holiday, the first for many years. 'Mrs G's good fortune also brought good luck for me. I'm going to enjoy myself,' he thought as he sniffed the fresh clean air.

Presently he came to the Quay and was soon in conversation with a fisherman. Learning that Bits and Pieces was a stranger to the district the man said, 'Two rivers meet

here, the Stour and the Avon. Wick Ferry's
over there, Hengistbury Head is straight in
front of you and the Priory lies to the left of
that lane, past Place Mill. There's a lot to see
here. It's very historic you know.'

'I'm sure it is,' said Bits and Pieces and,
thanking the man for the information, he
walked on. A line of swans glided proudly
towards him followed by a colony of hungry
ducks clamouring for food, their cries
resembling the cackling of witches, and he
made a resolve to bring some titbits for them
the next day.

On the sun-dappled waters small boats
bobbed gently while seagulls and cormorants
wheeled and swooped from above and in the
distance Hengistbury Head, stark and lonely,
brooded over secrets more than a thousand
years old.

As though in a dream, Bits and Pieces
wandered past the old mill where centuries

before monks had ground their corn and, crossing into the quiet gardens nestling below the Priory Church, he sat by the river.

An old man sitting at the other end of the seat wished him a cheery 'Good Morning', and asked if Bits and Pieces was a visitor. Learning that he was the old man proudly announced that he was one of the oldest inhabitants of Twynham. 'I was born here so were my father and grandfather. Pot Boilers all of us.'

'Pot Boilers?'

The old man laughed. 'I thought that would puzzle you. Would you like me to explain?'

'Yes I would.'

'Well, any householder living in the old borough of Twynham with an open fireplace where a pot can be boiled is a Pot Boiler and has Commoners' Rights. It means we can graze cattle or horses on certain tracts of common land. It's a privilige that was granted by the Lord of the Manor centuries ago.'

'Well I never!'

'I'll tell you another interesting thing.' He waved his arms in the direction of the Priory. 'There used to be a school up there in St Michael's Loft over the Lady Chapel. My grandfather went there and many's the tale he's told of the things the boys got up to. Best of all were his smuggling stories. I'd listen for hours.'

'Smuggling stories?'

'There was one about a boy – it was before Grandad's time of course – who saw from the schoolroom a column of smugglers surrounded by armed men riding along Hengistbury Head. I used to get very excited about that.'

He pulled out a large turnip watch. 'Time I was getting along. I've enjoyed our chat.'

'It was most interesting,' said Bits and Pieces.

He went back to the cottage to find Mrs

Goodheart busily turning out cupboards. 'Can't imagine what I'm going to do with all this stuff. Never seen so much,' she said pointing to piles of linen, china and glass.

'I expect you'll find a use for it,' said Bits and Pieces and knew that in spite of her offhand tone she was overwhelmed to find she now had so many possessions. All her life she had had so little, living in the draughty old cottage next to his. Surely now she would decide to move here and live out the rest of her days in comfort.

He sighed, knowing how much he would miss her for she was like a mother to him, cooking and cleaning while he was at work and accepting little in return for her care.

'What are you sighing for?'

'I was just thinking how much I shall miss you when you move here.'

'Haven't made up my mind yet what I'll do but there's one thing you can do, Bits and

Pieces – make a nice cup of tea.'

'I will and I'll put a bit of oil on that squeaky gate and a new washer on the bathroom tap.'

'Leave the odd jobs until tomorrow. I've found an album full of old photographs. We can look at it over tea.'

The sepia-tinted pictures spoke of a bygone age before the area around Twynham had been developed and showed how the district had once looked. 'I've also found some old books, local history, that sort of thing,' Mrs Goodheart went on.

'I'd like to read them. A man I was talking to said there's a lot to see here.'

Mrs Goodheart screwed up her face in an effort to recall something. 'As I told you, it's many, many years since I stayed here but I seem to remember Edith taking me to see a ruined castle or some such place. I know I got excited about something and it made Edith cross but I can't remember what it was.'

Bits and Pieces found plenty of jobs to do around the cottage in the next few days. Turning out the dusty loft was one of the worst for it was crammed full with old trunks, cases and boxes that Mrs Goodheart declared would take hours to go through.

Despite the work he found time to walk to the Quay every day and wander through the Priory Gardens. The ruins of the Castle and the Constable's house intrigued him and when at night he read accounts of the battles which

had been fought over them he marvelled that there was anything left of the buildings.

More exciting still were the smuggling stories told by the man next door. 'They were all at it,' Mr Kimmins said. 'Proper old carry on it were. All the inns seem to have been involved. People of quality too I shouldn't wonder. They say that some of the smugglers brought the brandy, tobacco and sichlike along a tunnel leading from the river to the Old George and sold it to the landlord.'

'They must have taken a terrible risk.'

''Course they did but they were poor, hungry and did what they did because they could see no other way of making a living. Of course it was agin the law and some of them paid dearly for it. There was often fighting and bloodshed when the Revenue Officers caught up with them.'

Bits and Pieces tried to tell the story to Mrs Goodheart that night but she took little notice and seemed strangely quiet. Thinking she was unwell he asked, 'Are you all right, Mrs G.?'

'Why shouldn't I be?'

'You look, well, sort of worried.'

For a moment she made no answer then handed him a slim note-book roughly bound in faded sailcloth. A few yellowing pages were covered with meaningless words written in a spiky hand.

'I can't make head nor tail of what's written inside and I don't think you will either,' she said.

A quick glance told the junk man she was right, yet though the senseless words meant nothing to him they roused feelings of excitement, reminding him of messages he and his school friends had written to each other; messages in code for fear they fell into the wrong hands.

He grinned. 'This is in some sort of code, Mrs G. I'd love to have a go at cracking it.'

'I don't know if we should. It may have been someone's private thoughts, Edith's perhaps.'

Bits and Pieces stared at the writing. 'Whoever wrote this did so years before your cousin was born.' He pointed to the letter S and Mrs Goodheart said slowly, 'If I let you do what you want will you promise me that you will never tell anyone other than me what you find?'

'You ought to know me better than that, Mrs G.'

'It's because I trust you that I'm letting you do it. It will also settle some doubts in my mind.'

'Doubts? What doubts?'

Mrs Goodheart rose from the table and, putting her hand on his shoulder, said earnestly, 'If you decipher that book I'll tell you, Jim. If you don't –' She shrugged her shoulders. 'Let's wait and see shall we? . . . '

THE CODE

IENDRV ISTH AYD YB OEYPVRT OT
OINJ AYDV ELBL ILWLAISHRR
ADN OESTHR IN OUIIGTWTTN ETH
EIEENXCSM. AYM ODG AEHV
EYMRC ON YM OULS.

ANJ 9 1785
IHWT AISHRR ELBL ADN OESTHR OT
HXC.
AEDLND EAT ADN IISSPRT.
IDWL ITNGH.

ANJ 16
AEDLND IEWN ADN IISSPRT OMFR
ETH EEB.
EYVR ODCL.

26

ANJ 30
EAEDSCP EEUERVN. OTW AOSWGN OEN ATCR
EIEDSZ. EDFR OOERCP OTSH IN EGL.

EBF 9

EEUERVN EEEDPRVNT UEYBTTRFL OMFR AIGLNDN.

EBF 20
AKDR ITNGH. UIEDBR ASCSK ON EAHHT.

EBF 21
ETS OUT IHWT AISHRR ADN ELBL OT OETCLLC ASCSK.
ETM EEUERVN. EAEDSCP IHWT ELBL. AISHRR ADN
OESTHR AUEDCPTR.
OWSN ADN EETSL.

AHMRC 5
AEDLND IEFV AESBL IKSL IISSPRT
ADN EAT.
ALL ELWL.
EYVR ODCL.

AHMRC 7
ETLF AYBRND ORF OOSDCTR EEF.

UILNT AUAYJNR NI ISTH EARY OF
OUR ODLR 1785 I ASW A ODG
EAIGFRN OERSB AIEAIGPLNDLN
ANM. YM OAECTTG ASW
OEYHNSTL OUTBGH IHWT EAISRNNG
OMFR YM AIGCLLN AS A
AOIGHRDWRKN IEANFSHRM.
IUAESCRCMSTNC ENTH
OEDFRC EM IONY UIGSMGGLN UTB I
ILWL AEHV ON OEMR OF IT
ORF I ILWL OTN EB A AYPRT OT
OOEDBLDSH ADN OEWRS.

Two   A frightening adventure

Bits and Pieces spent the evening trying to find the answer to the code. By bedtime he was no nearer a solution than he had been when he started, and, knowing he would be unable to sleep, went for a walk.

This was the time of day when he most missed his dog but while he was away Barney

was staying with his brothers. He wondered if
Barney missed him and if trade had picked up
in the junkyard. John had said that if things
didn't get better they would have to close
down. Everything seemed to be changing he
thought, what with Mrs G. moving away and
his brothers thinking of selling the junkyard.

How wonderful it would be if he could find
a hoard of gold or discover a work of art
worth millions, but things like that only
happened in books not in real life. He sighed,
quite forgetting he had once made a wonderful
discovery that had brought good fortune to an
old lady and a handsome new fishing rod for
himself.*

His thoughts returned to Mrs Goodheart
and the note-book she had found. Could it
have belonged to Edith's father, grandfather or

★Bits & Pieces solves a mystery

even great-grandfather he wondered and what had the writer wanted to hide? Mrs Goodheart had suggested private thoughts, a kind of diary, but also it might have been something to do with business.

A painting of Edith showed a tall, thin, pale-faced girl with a shy – or was it a secretive – look? Had she known what the code meant? Had somebody told her or had she deciphered it for herself?

He was so busy day-dreaming he did not notice where he was going until a thump inside his pocket made him stop. Moppy was trying to say something but the words were swept away by a howling wind and the boom and roar of the sea.

The startled junkman saw he was on a sandy beach only a few yards from the sea thundering towards him. All around was desolate waste and an eerie darkness that sent shivers up his spine. He dropped to his knees behind a boulder and hid his face inside his jacket. 'Where am I, Moppy? How did I get here?' he cried.

'The usual way – day-dreaming. I thought I'd cured you of that bad habit.' The voice was faint.

'But where am . . .'

With a mighty shriek the contemptuous wind swept him up and sent him sprawling into the surf. For a moment he lay helpless, too shocked to resist the relentless pull of the sea. Then as the giant waves tried to drag him further in he lurched to his feet and struggled gasping from the icy water.

As if to atone for its behaviour the wind suddenly dropped and a new sound came on the air, faint but unmistakable – the sound of a boat running ashore. Wretched in his sodden clothes, Bits and Pieces was deaf to all sounds as he tried to wipe the salt from his eyes. He had never known such misery, such cold.

All he could think about was getting back to the cottage and putting on some dry clothes when a flash of light and the sound of voices roused him. He peered into the darkness and, as his eyes became used to the gloom, saw a group of men at the water's edge.

More figures appeared and seemed to be standing in a large, open boat. Then he felt himself pushed forward, a spade was thrust into his hands and a voice urged him to dig 'and be quick about it!'

As though in a dream he did as he was told. Others joined in and working fast and in silence they soon dug a deep hole. Casks were then lowered into it and covered with sand and shingle.

A watery moon suddenly peeped out and by its light Bits and Pieces saw a wagon being loaded with chests and kegs. A shiver of fear ran through him at the sight of an armed man sitting at the front of the vehicle and another at the back.

Someone swore about the light and orders were given to speed up the work as more wagons appeared. The men worked unceasingly until at last the boat, empty of its cargo, slipped away. Then, one by one, the men seemed to melt into the landscape until only Bits and Pieces was left.

'Come on – it's time to go,' Moppy squeaked.

The junk man put his hand inside his jacket.

To his surprise it was dry! He felt his shirt and trousers – they too were dry. 'I don't understand. I was wet through,' he cried.

'So you were and it served you right,' said Moppy.

'You must have been wet too,' Bits and Pieces retorted. The mop laughed. 'My magic kept me dry. So would you have been if you hadn't daydreamed. Artemisia didn't mean you to nearly drown yourself.'

'Artemisia!' Bits and Pieces stood motionless, his mind in a whirl as the first fingers of light stole across the sky. The colours changed, deepening through azure, blues and gold until the sun burst through bathing him in a light so brilliant that he was forced to close his eyes.

When he opened them he was back in the cottage and the Priory clock was chiming midnight.

Safe in his room he re-lived his adventure

and knew that Artemisia had kept her promise 'that through her he would learn many things'. Her magic had taken him back in time to a smuggling raid in the late eighteenth century, a raid that Mr Kimmins had described earlier that week.

Bits and Pieces had been one of the 'landers' helping to unload what must have been tea, spirits and tobacco from the boat which the 'runners' who knew every inch of the coast for miles around had brought safely ashore. What had happened to them he wondered? Had they been caught by Excise Officers or had the smuggled goods been delivered to a place of safety – an inn, the crypt of a church or an isolated farm?

He yawned and too weary to think any more began to undress.

He woke early next morning thinking he had had a bad dream until aching muscles reminded him of the night before. He looked at the mop lying on the bedside table and saw it was grinning. 'It's kind of Artemisia to give me these adventures but I wish they were not so uncomfortable,' he grumbled.

'Being uncomfortable was entirely your own fault. If you hadn't been day-dreaming you wouldn't have gone so near to the sea or been seen by the smugglers and made to work. Be thankful that they thought you were one of their own men,' Moppy retorted.

Bits and Pieces shivered. 'I don't mind admitting I was frightened when I saw those armed men.'

'Most people would have been scared if they had seen what you did.'

'The strange thing is that I didn't even hear them coming, Moppy. That's why it was such a shock to see them.'

'They covered the ponies' hooves and harness with sacking so they couldn't be heard. They didn't want any sound to attract attention.'

'And I don't want to hear another word about smuggling as long as I live,' said Bits and Pieces . . .

Three   Danny

Mrs Goodheart was preparing dinner when a loud thump on the front door followed by a voice calling, 'It's me, Danny Black. Can I come in?' announced the arrival of a tall sandy-haired youth about eighteen years old, dressed in an assortment of garments that looked like leftovers from a jumble sale.

Mrs Goodheart stared in surprise as the stranger walked in and kissed her on both cheeks. 'You must be dear Aunt Edith's cousin, Abigail Goodheart. I'm Danny Black, Aunt Edith's godson. That makes us kind of related doesn't it? Can I . . . may I call you Aunt Abby?'

His blue eyes widened and his face crinkled into a smile of such sweetness that Mrs Goodheart liked him on sight. 'Did you say Black? Danny Black?'

'The same. I took Aunt Edith's name you see. She wanted to adopt me – make me her lawful son and heir but then we had a little misunderstanding and things were never the same after that. Never mind . . . what's past is past. No-one can undo what has happened. In fact I never thought to see this place again.' He looked round the cottage as if memorising everything in the room. 'When I heard that you had moved in, Aunt Abby, I felt I must see you and wish you every happiness in my old – in your new home.'

'You mean THIS was your home! You expected to go on living here?'

Danny looked away. 'You're not to worry about me, Aunt Abby. I shall be all right. I have friends you know, but if you'd allow me to call on you sometimes just to talk about the old days . . . about Aunt Edith.'

'We'd better start now over a cup of coffee. Sit down, Danny.'

If Bits and Pieces was surprised to see the strange looking lad when he returned from shopping, Danny was equally surprised to see him. 'I . . . I thought you were here by yourself, Aunt Abby,' he exclaimed.

'I wouldn't be here if it wasn't for my kind neighbour, Bits and Pieces. He brought me down and is staying while I sort things out.'

'Bits and . . . That's a funny sort of name, isn't it?'

'My real name's Jim – Jim Smith. I'm called Bits and Pieces because I collect bits and pieces of junk.'

'I'm Danny Black. Aunt Edith's godson.'

'Pleased to meet you,' said Bits and Pieces and shook Danny's limp hand.

'Yes, well, I suppose it's time I went. Mustn't outstay my welcome.'

'You'll do nothing of the sort. You'll stay and have a bit of dinner with us, Danny. It won't be long and while I'm in the kitchen you

two can have a nice chat,' Mrs Goodheart said
as she bustled out of the room.

There was silence for a moment then Bits
and Pieces asked, 'Do you live in Twynham?'

'I used to live in this cottage until Aunt
Edith and I fell out.'

'I'm sorry.'

'Me too. It was silly to argue over
something so trivial that I've forgotten what it
was. What about you? Are you going to live
here with Aunt Abby?'

'No, and I don't know yet if she is.'

Danny looked surprised. 'Is there some
doubt about it?'

'I don't know what she's going to do and I
don't believe she does either.'

'I see.'

The words, spoken softly seemed to hang
on the air making Bits and Pieces strangely
uneasy. Then, as if he had come to a sudden
decision, Danny said, 'I might as well tell you,

that is, just in case . . . so you can be
prepared . . .'

'If you've something to say for goodness
sake say it!'

'It's about this place, Cockleshell Cottage.

Did you know it's haunted?'

Bits and Pieces raised a warning finger. 'Not so loud. I don't want Mrs Goodheart to hear.'

Danny looked nervously at the kitchen door. 'I've never actually seen the man but I've heard noises – in the cellar.'

'Man! What man? What cellar? There isn't a cellar here.'

'Yes there is. Not that there's anything in it apart from spiders which is why Aunt Edith never used the place. There's a trap door behind the bottom of the stairs.'

'I've never seen it.'

'I'm not surprised. It's a dark corner.'

'And this man – this ghost – who is he?'

'Some say he's a fisherman who was drowned at sea, others, that he was a smuggler. How true it is . . . ' Danny shrugged his shoulders.

'You say you've never seen him but you've heard noises. What kind of noises?'

'It's hard to say. Creaks, muffled footsteps, tappings.'

'All houses make noises like that especially old houses.'

Mrs Goodheart hurried in. 'Dinner's ready. Set the table, Bits and Pieces. Danny can help me bring in the food.'

The delicious meal, for Mrs Goodheart was an excellent cook, was made more enjoyable for her by their unexpected guest. Danny proved to be an entertaining companion with a fund of amusing stories which delighted Mrs Goodheart but Bits and Pieces, uneasy at the thought of a ghost in the cottage, hardly listened.

A sudden noise startled Mrs Goodheart. 'What's that?' she exclaimed.

'It's nothing. Only a door banging.'

'It's the old smuggler come to haunt . . .' Danny clapped a hand over his mouth and an expression of dismay spread over his face.

'Idiot! Fathead!'

'I'm sorry. I didn't mean to say anything. It sort of slipped out.'

'What slipped out?'

Danny stared helplessly at Bits and Pieces as Mrs Goodheart, pale and determined, said again, 'What didn't you mean to say, Danny?'

'That . . . That this cottage is haunted – haunted by an old smuggler.'

Something in the way he said it made the hairs rise on the back of Bits and Pieces' neck. 'Rubbish! Absolute rubbish!' he stormed.

'It's not rubbish. I've seen him myself. So did Aunt Edith. An old man with an evil face.'

Mrs Goodheart shuddered and Bits and Pieces shouted, 'That's not what you told me. You said you'd never seen a ghost. You'd only heard noises.'

'I could see I'd upset you so I pretended I hadn't seen anything.'

'You also said if there was a ghost it could be

the ghost of a fisherman drowned at sea.'

'Fisherman, smuggler, what's the difference? Lots of ghost stories are old wives tales anyway,' Danny said cheerfully. 'Perhaps this one is.'

'How can you say that when you've just told us you've seen the ghost,' Bits and Pieces said sharply.

'Oh dear! I was only trying to cheer you up . . . to make amends. I wish now I'd never said anything.'

He looked so woebegone that Mrs Goodheart patted his arm. 'It was right to tell me, Danny. Better I know what there is to know before I start putting down new roots.'

'P'rhaps the ghost won't come again,' Danny said.

'He'd better not,' Bits and Pieces muttered.

Soon afterwards, Danny left and Bits and Pieces at once set about reassuring Mrs

Goodheart. To his surprise she refused to discuss the story of the ghost, saying what was more important was the unfair treatment Danny had received from her cousin.

'Telling him she was going to leave the cottage to him and then leaving it to me. That was a cruel thing to do.'

'I expect your cousin had her reasons.'

'It was still an unkind act – breaking a promise like that. It makes me feel I should make the cottage over to Danny. I don't need it. I have got a home of my own while he, poor boy, is living in one room and paying an enormous rent.'

'I shouldn't do anything in a hurry, Mrs G. Think about it. After all you don't know anything about him except what he's told you.'

'I believe every word he's said. You can see by his face he's an honest boy and I don't need you to tell me what to do. I shall make up my

own mind and do what I think is right,' Mrs
Goodheart snapped.

She had never spoken so sharply to Bits and
Pieces but he did not argue with her for fear
she would think *he* wanted something for
himself. He glanced out of the window. 'It's
not completely dark yet so I think I'll have a
walk unless of course there is anything I can do
for you, Mrs G.'

'Nothing, thank you,' she said coldly and
going into the kitchen closed the door firmly
behind her.

Mrs Goodheart's bad mood had gone by the
time Bits and Pieces returned and they spent a
pleasant evening watching an old film on
television. A coal fire had been lit, for the
weather had turned chilly, and long after she
had gone to bed he continued to sit by it while
he tried to unravel the secret of the little book
Mrs Goodheart had found.

As before he could make no sense of it and

was on the point of giving up when Moppy cried, 'Use your brains as well as your eyes, Bits and Pieces.'

Again the junk man looked at the writing but it still did not make sense. 'Say the letters aloud and think!' Moppy said fiercely.

'IENDRV ISTH AYD YB OEYPVRT OT OINJ.'

'Now tell me what you've discovered; what your teeny-weeny brain has told you.'

Bits and Pieces stared blankly at the writing then began tracing the letters with his forefinger. Instantly, he saw something he had not seen before. 'Every word begins with a vowel, that is, nearly every word.'

'Good. Now all you've got to do is put the letters in order.'

'That's easier said than done.'

'Start with an easy one – a short one.'

Once more, Bits and Pieces looked at the page. 'The third is day and the fourth is by but

I don't think it's as easy as all that.' As he
spoke the letters OINJ seemed to rearrange
themselves. 'It's join join!' he said excitedly.

'So now you know how its done – or do
you?' Moppy asked.

'I think I do. The vowel came first, then the
last letter followed by the other two. Won't
Mrs G. be surprised when . . . ' He stopped

abruptly, suddenly aware that someone was watching him. For a moment he was too shocked to move. Then rushing to the window he flung aside the curtains; the window was open and from the street came the sound of someone running away . . .

Four   Magic

'Did you open the window yesterday?' Bits and Pieces asked next morning.

Mrs Goodheart looked indignant. 'Open the window? Of course I didn't! It was much too cold – that's why I lit the fire. Wait a minute tho' I remember now. I did open it. The chimney smoked and I wanted to clear the air.'

'It was left open,' Bits and Pieces said sternly.

'No it wasn't. Danny closed it for me.'

'He couldn't have done. He left before I went out and you lit the fire while I was gone.'

'He came back. Didn't I tell you? Brought me those nice daffodils to make up for upsetting me yesterday. Wasn't that kind of him? He's working away for a few days so he won't be coming again until after the weekend.'

'He didn't close the window properly. It was wide open when I found it.'

'He must have thought it was all right because he drew the curtains.'

Bits and Pieces glared at the daffodils and longed to say what he thought about someone stupid enough to leave a window unfastened. 'It's as good as inviting a burglar in,' he muttered and instantly remembered the sound of footsteps running away.

Had someone seen the open window and intended to get in? There were plenty of things in the cottage worth stealing. Or had that someone seen him working on the old notebook and been curious about it? Could it hold the key to a treasure trove or a missing heirloom? Did someone know its secret?'

If only he had been quick enough to see who it was and smart enough to capture the man. Then perhaps Mrs Goodheart would pay more attention to him and not be so full of Danny.

It wasn't that he had anything against the lad other than blurting out that stupid ghost story. On the contrary, he seemed nice enough, thoughtful too, buying those flowers for Mrs G. It was something he, Bits and Pieces, had meant to do when he'd gone shopping the other day but he'd forgotten. If he bought any now it would look as though he was copying Danny and he wouldn't like Mrs G. to think that. 'I suppose I should thank him. Those flowers put her in a good mood,' Bits and Pieces thought as he carried the breakfast dishes to the sink.

'Do you mind if I leave you to do the washing up? I want to go out for a little while,' Mrs Goodheart called.

'Of course I don't.' It was the first time she had left the cottage since their arrival and Bits and Pieces could not help wondering where she was going. He had tried several times to persuade her to go for a walk but she always

had an excuse for staying indoors. Now she
was going out of her own accord. It couldn't
be to do any shopping, he always did that; and
it couldn't be to visit anyone because she didn't
know anyone in Twynham except Mr
Kimmins and Mr Dewar, Cousin Edith's
solicitor.

Solicitor! That was where she had gone – to
see the solicitor; to tell him she wanted to give
the cottage to Danny because she felt he had
been unfairly treated by his Godmother. Bits
and Pieces stared at the soapsuds in the bowl
and thought about kind, trusting Mrs
Goodheart who saw nothing but good in a
young man she hardly knew. Maybe she was
right. Maybe Danny was all she thought him
to be but Bits and Pieces could not help
wishing they knew a little more about him.

He would have questioned Mr Kimmins but
he had gone away. Since there was no-one else
he could ask, for the other cottages in the

terrace were let only to summer visitors, he was forced to push his doubts to the back of his mind and think about something else.

Mrs Goodheart returned to find Bits and Pieces working on the book. 'Found the answer yet?' she asked.

'I'm getting on.'

She took off her hat and speared it with a long hatpin. Bits and Pieces looked away. 'You're going to stick that in your head one of these days.'

'Don't be silly. Of course I won't.'

'Well don't say I didn't warn you.'

'Stop fussing and make us a nice cup of tea. One of your specials, Bits and Pieces.'

While he waited for the kettle to boil, Bits and Pieces thought of all the questions he would have liked to ask Mrs Goodheart and tried to guess the answers she would have given. This had a bad effect on the teamaking for he poured boiling water in the milk jug and

filled the pot with tea and cold milk.

'You are an idiot,' Mrs Goodheart said crossly when she saw what he had done. 'Since we've been here you've made cocoa with gravy powder, left shopping on a park seat and now this. It's time you stopped day-dreaming and concentrated on what you're doing.'

A stifled laugh came from Bits and Pieces' jacket.

'What's that?' Mrs Goodheart asked suspiciously.

'I didn't hear anything but I'll look outside if you like.'

'While you're about it you can fetch a nice, crusty loaf from that little bakers but be sure to bring it back with you.'

'I will.'

Bits and Pieces came out of the bakers and turned into the High Street. Despite an icy wind scores of people were standing about and the road, jammed with carts, wagons and other horse-drawn vehicles was impossible to cross. Puzzled, he stared around and shivered inside his light jacket. 'Suffering sausages! The sun was shining when I came out,' he exclaimed.

It was a few moments before he noticed the absence of cars or saw anything unusual about his surroundings. Now, instead of a terrace of shops he was surprised to see houses, some small and thatched, others large and stone built with fine porticos and ornate railings. Further down the road were poorer dwellings, a few shops and an inn where a large crowd had gathered.

Most of the people looked poor and shabby; the women in long, threadbare skirts with woollen shawls over their heads while the men's homespun jerseys and rough trousers were tattered and sea-stained.

A man wearing a long, linen smock and gaiters and armed with a stick tried to force a way through for his cattle, and, seeing him, the crowds parted only to come together again as if drawn into a secret assembly. Bits and Pieces felt an overwhelming desire to know what they were saying and a thrill of delight ran through him when he heard the mop's muffled voice. 'Artemisia has made you invisible. Listen! but do not talk.'

Artemisia! He should have guessed that this was her doing. That he was in a time-slip, seeing Twynham as it was long ago and he marvelled at the ease with which she could spirit him back into the past.

'What shall I discover this time, Moppy,' he whispered excitedly.

'Plenty if you remember what you hear.'

Stepping carefully into the frosty road, Bits and Pieces squeezed between stationary vehicles to reach the Inn on the opposite side where a man reading aloud from a page of newsprint was being heckled by the crowd.

'Speak up!'

'Read it slowly.'

'Go back to the beginning.'

'We can't understand a word you say.'

A murmur of approval greeted these remarks causing angry words with the reader before he agreed to start again. Bits and Pieces listened intently as with much hemming and hawing the man began.

'*HAMPSHIRE CHRONICLE JANUARY 1786. Winchester, Saturday January 28.*

WINCHESTER. SATURDAY Jan 28.
George Coombes who in June feffion was convicted of being aiding and abetting in the murder of W.
Allen, late mafter of the Sloop Oreftes in the harbour of Chriftchurch. who. on information of
there being fmuggled goods on fhore, manned his
boat. in order to proceed on fhore. but the boat
ftriking on the fand he got into the water to fet
her afloat, when a ball from a gun on fhore fhot
him. of which he died; the verdict was left
fpecial for the opinion of the fudges. which
beingdelivered by Mr. Juftice Willes.the prif-
oner received fentence to be executed on
Tuefday morning at Execution dock.
　　He went out of Newgate at a quarter paff 12
o'clock attended by the proper Admiralty
Officers and the filveroar carried before him
He behaved with that decency which became
his untimely end.
　The body of the above unfortunate young
fellowis ordered by the Court of Admiralty
b be hung in chainsnear Chriftchurch har-
bur, where the act was committed.

HAMPSHIRE CHRONICLE JAN 1786

George Coombes, who in June sessions was
convicted of being aiding and abetting in the
murder of W. Allen, late master of the sloop
Orestes, in the harbour of Christchurch, who,
on information of there being smuggled goods

on shore, manned his boat, in order to proceed on shore, but the boat striking on the sand, he got into the water to set her afloat, when a ball from a gun on shore, shot him, of which he died; the verdict was left special for the opinion of the judges, which being delivered by Mr Justice Willes, the prisoner received sentence to be executed on Tuesday morning at Execution Dock . . . '

'What about John Streeter? Why ain't he alongside George Coombes?' a man interrupted.

'They'll never catch him. Reckon he's gone to ground in Guernsey,' another shouted.

A sharp faced woman shook her fist angrily. 'Like it or not, Revenue men won't keep him away. He'll be back to see his wife and children.'

'What about the others? Will Harris, Davy Bell, Amos Brown, Fred Cooper, and the rest,' screamed a fat woman.

Absorbed in what was being said, Bits and Pieces moved nearer the speakers. In his haste he caught one man a glancing blow and trod on another's foot. Instantly there was uproar as first one and then another blamed his neighbour for the injury he had received. The argument soon developed into a fight and Bits and Pieces turned tail and fled.

He stopped as he reached the Priory and loosened his jacket. The icy wind had vanished and the air felt soft and warm. 'Nice evening,' said a passer by.

'Lovely!' said Bits and Pieces and knew in that instant that the magic which had made him invisible had gone. He turned and stared down Church Street and saw he was back in the twentieth century . . .

Five   A secret revealed

With the loaf safely delivered to Mrs Goodheart, Bits and Pieces pleaded a headache and went for a walk. He needed time to think, to put his thoughts in some kind of order and, most of all, to remember what he had heard.

He walked towards Druitt Gardens, repeating the names of men, obviously smugglers, who had been named by the crowd so long ago: George Coombes, John Streeter, Bill, no Will Harris, somebody Bell, Fred Cooper and . . . and.' There was one other. He shook his head as if the action would jolt his memory but his mind remained a blank.

Again he recited the names and felt a child again, reciting nursery rhymes to his parents; 'George Coombes, John Streeter, Will Harris, Davy, Davy Bell, Fred Cooper, and . . .

and . . .' The last name was on the tip of his tongue and, fearing he would forget the others, he stopped to write them down.

Daylight faded into twilight bringing blackbirds, thrushes, robins and sparrows back to their nests. Oblivious of the gathering darkness, Bits and Pieces sat deep in thought until a lively wind, whisking, frisking through the trees made leaves and bushes quiver and dance in a madcap fashion. It ruffled his hair bringing him out of his trance–like state and he yawned and stretched his arms.

'As soon as Mrs G. is in bed I'll have another go at that code,' he said aloud.

In the early hours of the following morning, Bits and Pieces put down his pen and grinned at himself in the mirror. 'Well, well! Who'd believe that I'd be clever enough to uncover a secret like this?' he chuckled. He looked again at the faded writing and felt a pang of sympathy for the unknown scribe, as he read:

Driven this day by poverty to join Davy Bell,
Will Harris and others in outwitting the
Excisemen. May God have mercy on my soul.

Jan 9 1785
With Harris, Bell and others to XCH
Landed tea and spirits
Wild night.

Jan 16
Landed wine and spirits from the Bee.
very cold.

Jan 30
Escaped Revenue. Two wagons, one cart
seized. Fred Cooper shot in leg.

Feb 9
Revenue prevented Butterfly from landing.

Feb 20
Dark night. Buried casks on Heath.

Feb 21
Set out with Harris and Bell to collect
casks. Met Revenue. Escaped with Bell.
Harris and others captured.
Snow and sleet.

March 5
Landed five bales silk, spirits and tea.
All well.
Very cold.

March 7
Left brandy for Doctor's fee.

The entries occupied the first nine pages. On
the tenth in scribble which Bits and Pieces had
found difficult to decipher was written:

Until January in this year of our Lord 1785
I was a God fearing, sober, plaindealing man.

My cottage was honestly bought with earnings from my calling as a hardworking fisherman.

Circumstances then forced me into smuggling but I will have no more of it for I will not be a party to bloodshed and worse.

Bits and Pieces felt an overwhelming desire to know who the writer was. Before he had had time to realise what he was doing he had ripped the sailcloth from the cover.

'Suffering sausages! Whatever will Mrs G. say?' he groaned. For a moment he could not bear to see what he had done but his spirits soared when he looked at the damp-spotted paper and read:

STRICTLY PRIVATE

. . . . .AMOS BROWN – HIS BOOK.

Amos Brown, the name he could not remember! Some of the other names the fat woman had screamed out were also here in Amos Brown's writing. But why had the book been hidden in Cockleshell Cottage? Who was Amos Brown?

'Here's another riddle for you. When did brown become black?' Moppy called.

'I don't know.'

'You're not trying.'

'I don't want to. I'm too busy thinking about something important.'

'You'll be sorry.'

Something in the mop's voice made Bits and Pieces repeat the question. 'When did brown become black? When something brown was dyed black I suppose.'

'It's not the right answer.'

'Then I give up.'

'When Miss Brown married Mr Black.'

'What's that supposed to prove?'

'You're so thick, Bits and Pieces. Think!'

It was easier said than done and seeking inspiration the junk man fixed his eyes on Edith's portrait, pale, shy, secretive Edith . . . Edith . . . Edith Black! 'You mean Edith's mother was a Miss Brown?'

'No I don't.'

'So the book is nothing to do with her family. You heard Mrs G. say that the Blacks have lived here for almost two hundred years.'

'No she didn't! She said Edith's family have lived here all that time.'

'What's the difference?'

With an angry snort the mop flew across the room and hovered over the bookcase. 'See for yourself. The answer's here, stupid!'

Angry at being called stupid, Bits and Pieces was about to grab the mop when a muffled bang attracted his attention. At first he thought a cat had knocked over something in the garden but when the noise, which seemed to come from the cellar, continued at regular intervals he knew no animal was responsible for it. Could it be the ghost he wondered, and instantly dismissed the idea. The sounds he had heard were not the least bit ghostly . . .

Six   An old story

As suddenly as it had started the noise ceased, intensifying the silence which followed. Bits and Pieces ran into the kitchen, pulled aside the curtains and peered out. At first he could see nothing but as his eyes grew accustomed to the darkness he thought he saw someone run across the garden.

'That was no ghost,' he said grimly and rushed outside but he was too late; the figure had vanished.

Back in the kitchen he struggled to unbolt the trap door and went down into the cellar. It smelt dank and musty and his torch hardly penetrated the gloom but something told him it was empty and satisfied he returned to the living room. He stood there frowning, trying to remember what he had been doing before the noise started.

'Think hard!' Moppy cried and instantly Bits and Pieces remembered. He went to the bookcase and took out the first book he saw, Edith's Family Bible, and opened it quickly. Inside the front cover was a family tree. At the

Amos Brown   m   Agatha Webb

Clara
b 1784
d 1844
m
William Black

John
b 1805
d 1855
m
Alice Reed

Thomas
b 1832
d 1872
m
Hannah West

William   Henry   John Thomas
b 1834   b 1836   b 1840
d 1883   d 1881   d 1841
m   m
Emily Davis   Kate White

George
b 1873
d 1950
m
Mary Thomas

Edith
b 1905

head was the name AMOS BROWN husband
of Agatha Webb whose only daughter Clara
had married William Black. A list of children
born to succeeding members of the same
family ended with the name EDITH BLACK!

So Edith was descended from a smuggler!
Bits and Pieces could not help smiling at the
thought of such a respectable looking woman
being connected, however far back, with
someone who had broken the law. 'Well,
who'd have thought it!' he exclaimed. 'Wait
'til I tell Mrs G.'

'What will you tell me?' Mrs Goodheart
demanded. Her voice, so unexpected, made
him start and he swung round angrily. 'You
made me jump.'

'You woke me up – all that banging about.
Whatever have you been doing?'

'It wasn't me it was . . . it was a cat,' he
said, anxious not to alarm her.

'H'm. Sounded like several cats to me.' She

looked at the table. 'Are you still messing about with that old book? Haven't you been to bed yet?'

'One thing at a time,' said Bits and Pieces. 'Sit down and I'll tell you what I've discovered.'

A look of concern crossed her face as if she was expecting to hear something unpleasant. 'Don't look like that. It's nothing to worry about. It's funny really. Edith looking so correct and all that. Did you know she was descended from a smuggler?'

'There's nothing funny about that.'

'Come off it, Mrs G. If the truth's known lots of people are descended from smugglers, even worse perhaps.' Seeing the distress on her face he added quickly, 'Not that Edith's forebear was a bad man. On the contrary, Amos Brown was a hard-working fisherman who bought this cottage with money honestly earned. He says poverty forced him into smuggling but that didn't last long. Seems he refused to be involved in bloodshed and got out.'

He pushed the notebook and decoded papers across to her. 'It's all there. You can read it for yourself.'

Mrs Goodheart leant forward and stirred the still red embers in the grate. 'Now I'll tell *you* something, Bits and Pieces. When I was a little girl my father told me Edith's family were descended from a smuggler. It upset me very much. After all we were related and I believed that smugglers and pirates were as bad as one another. Still do in fact. They were all law-breakers, some even murderers.

'When father saw how distressed I was he said he'd only been teasing, he'd made it up, which was a great relief I can tell you. But ever since I heard that Edith had left me this cottage I've been worried about that old story. Did father make it up or was there any truth in it?

I've been still more bothered since I found that little book. You see I was afraid it might reveal that this cottage was bought with ill gotten gains. You don't know what a comfort it is to know it wasn't.'

'I can't see what you were worried about.'

'You will think I'm very foolish, Bits and Pieces, but if I thought this cottage or anything in it had been bought with money dishonestly obtained I wouldn't accept it.'

'You what!'

'I mean it. I couldn't . . . I wouldn't.'

She looked like a cartoon drawing of Britannia, sitting there in her dressing gown, the poker held like a sceptre, a look of indignation on her face and he could not help smiling.

'I know you're laughing at me. You think I'm a silly old woman.'

'No I don't. I think you're a very nice, honest woman, Mrs G. and it's time to stop

talking and go to bed.'

She put down the poker. 'You're right. It is.
Thank you for everything, Bits and Pieces.
You must have spent hours on that book.'

'What are you going to do with it, Mrs G.?'

'Burn it, I suppose. What else should I do
with it?'

'Leave it in your will to the Red House

Museum. It's a jolly good one and I'm sure they'd like to have it. After all, that little book is a bit of local history.'

'I'm sure you're right, Bits and Pieces. I'll do as you say. Goodnight.'

She went upstairs, leaving him to put out the lights. He took the mop from the bookcase where it had been hiding. 'That's one mystery settled, Moppy.'

'You wouldn't have done it without me.'

'I might have done. Now, what about these noises?'

'Work it out for yourself,' the mop said tartly and went back inside the junk man's pocket . . .

Seven   The intruder

The first thing Bits and Pieces saw when he returned from shopping the next day was a large box of chocolates tied with a pink bow. 'I see Danny's been,' he said.

Mrs Goodheart looked pleased. 'What a generous boy he is, so kind too. I had a bad headache and he insisted on making me a cup of tea while I rested. Wouldn't allow me near the kitchen. Said he was sorry to miss you but he had to get back. He's helping a friend in an antique shop.'

Feeling strangely disgruntled, the junk man went into the kitchen to make tea for himself. 'Danny, Danny, all I hear is Danny,' he muttered.

'You're jealous,' said Moppy.

'Don't be silly! Of course I'm not.'

'Then use your eyes, Bits and Pieces.'

However it was the junk man's nose that told him something was amiss. A faint but unmistakable smell, pungent, oily, coming from the trap door, and he saw two well-oiled bolts had been pulled from their sockets.

He stared hard, remembering how difficult it had been to open the trap door. Someone had now made it easy. Who was it? It was unthinkable that it could be Mrs Goodheart. The only other likely person was Danny!

Mystified, he secured the trap door, made some tea and tried to read the paper but all he could think about was Danny. 'I've never really trusted him. All that toadying to Mrs G.,' he muttered angrily.

But why should Danny have taken the trouble to oil the bolts? What interest could there be in an empty cellar? He could only get into it from inside the cottage and how could he do that without someone knowing?

Bits and Pieces knew there was only one way to find out. He would leave the trap door as he had found it, unbolted, and keep watch after Mrs Goodheart had gone to bed.

He spent the rest of the day wondering if he should tell her what he had discovered. Against the desire to prepare her for a late visitor was the stronger wish not to alarm her and in the end he decided to say nothing.

It was well after midnight when he heard the first sounds of an intruder. His heart beat fast at the thought that it might not be the one he expected but someone violent, someone who might . . . He shook his head, angry with himself and listened again as the sounds came nearer; slow, cautious steps followed by the creak and crack of old wood. Now the sound of something being moved stealthily, then silence as if the intruder was listening too.

Bits and Pieces held his breath, fearful that he might be heard, and peeped through the curtains. A moment later a shadowy figure slipped into the room. Something clicked and a beam of light shone out, illuminating the papers on the table. A hand tossed them aside and grabbed Amos Brown's book. Bits and Pieces took a deep breath, switched on his torch and stared at Danny Black.

For a moment neither spoke then, 'Why, Danny? Why?'

Immediately, Danny began making excuses. 'How would you like it if someone told you you'd got to get out of your home? Aunt Edith said she was leaving me this cottage so why should I believe what the solicitor says? How do I know he's speaking the truth? Why hasn't he found the right will? Everyone's against me including Mr Kimmins. He's never liked me since his cat got kicked. Wasn't my fault if the cat got in the way of my foot, was it?'

'But why steal that old book?'

'I wanted to know what was in it, that's why. It was on the table one day when I called and Aunt Abby made a great business pushing it out of sight. It made me think it was something important. Then one night I watched you reading it and writing things down and I wondered if it was anything to do with me; if it could prove that I am the rightful owner here.'

Bits and Pieces sighed wearily. 'You're not, Danny. Nobody's done you out of anything.'

'Why should I believe you? You're no better than the rest. People are always promising to help me, to do things for me, then letting me down and blaming me when things go wrong. It's not fair.'

'That's no reason for frightening Mrs Goodheart with your tales of ghosts.'

'I hoped she would let me come and live with her until you said you didn't know if she was going to live here. It seemed the next best thing would be to tell her about the ghost and scare her away. It isn't easy to sell a haunted property but I would have offered to rent the cottage, cheaply of course. Now everything's gone wrong. You'll hand me over to the police I suppose and it's not my fault I'm in this mess.'

'Let him go. Just let him go,' Mrs Goodheart said quietly. Their voices had

wakened her and coming downstairs she had
heard enough to realise that Danny was not the
kind, helpful young man she had thought him
to be. Without looking at him she turned away
and went back upstairs.

'It's not fair – it wasn't my fault,' Danny
whined and flinging open the front door he ran
out. Bits and Pieces promptly bolted it,
secured the trap door, heated some milk and
took it up to Mrs Goodheart.

'Drink this and go to sleep. There's nothing
to worry about, Mrs G. We can talk about
Danny in the morning.'

'There's nothing to say and don't tell anyone
about tonight. Don't even think of it.'

'I won't,' Bits and Pieces promised. Yet as
he lay in bed he could not help feeling sorry for
Danny who had lost so much and wondered
what would become of him . . .

Eight   Mrs Goodheart decides

Mr Kimmins returned home the next day and
seeing him in the garden, Bits and Pieces took
the opportunity to ask about the ghost in
Cockleshell Cottage.

'Ghost? What ghost?'

'The ghost of the smuggler or is it a
fisherman?'

'Whoever told you that load of old rubbish?'

'You mean there's no truth in it?'

'Of course there isn't! The only ghost in
these parts is one reputed to be in the
Priory – Prior Draper, but few have seen him.
Who told you there was one next door?'

'Danny.'

'Danny Black?'

'Yes.'

'If you believe what he says you'll believe
anything.'

Bits and Pieces was shocked. 'You mean he's a liar?'

'He's that and worse. He wants the easy life and someone else to provide it. He was sure Miss Black would leave him the cottage; so she might have done if she hadn't found him with his fingers in her purse and discovered he'd been robbing her for ages.'

'I can't believe it!'

Mr Kimmins scowled. 'You'd better. Edith threw him out but he was soon back whining he was in trouble with the police and how sorry he was and he'd never do it again. But it was too late. Edith had already altered her will and left everything to her cousin. She told me what she had done and I was very pleased. I never trusted that Danny.'

'He was taking a chance telling us such a cock and bull story. He must have known I'd ask you about the ghost, that sooner or later we'd discover the truth.'

'That's where Master Danny thought he was being clever. You see I always go away at this time of the year. I stay with my daughter until all the visitors have gone home – can't stand crowds. It might have been months before Mrs Goodheart learnt that her cottage is ghost free.

'As it happens, my grandsons have gone down with measles so I thought I'd make myself scarce and come home for a couple of weeks. It will make things easier for Mary.'

Scarcely able to take in all he had heard, Bits and Pieces went indoors. Two things were uppermost in his mind; to make sure Mrs Goodheart never learnt the whole truth about Danny and to go into the cellar and find out how he had got in.

This time he made a thorough search and discovered a hole in the wall led to the unoccupied cottage on the other side. Seeing this Bits and Pieces knew it must be reported.

A policeman soon arrived. 'Whoever made that hole got in through the kitchen window next door but we won't know if anything's missing until we get in touch with the owner. It's always a problem with holiday homes.

Unless we're told we don't know whether anyone is living in a property or not.'

He looked keenly at Bits and Pieces. 'It took some time to knock out those bricks, several visits in fact, but how he hoped to get through that trap door . . . ' Puzzled, he shook his head. 'Surely you heard him banging about. You must have done.'

'We've only been here a few days. The cottage has been empty since Miss Black died. We did hear a noise last night but . . . ' Bits and Pieces hesitated as he saw Mrs Goodheart looking at him. 'No, we didn't see anyone. We really can't help you.'

'Well thanks for reporting the break in and please keep your eyes open in case chummy returns.'

'Chummy?' Mrs Goodheart repeated.

The policeman smiled. 'Perhaps I should have said intruder.'

No sooner had the door closed behind him than Mrs Goodheart said, 'Let's go home, Bits and Pieces. As soon as we can.'

'What about this place?'

'I'd already decided to sell it. Some of the furniture and other things too. I've seen

Edith's solicitor, he's going to arrange
everything for me. I shall spend the money I
get on my old cottage, make it more
comfortable.'

'Are you sure that's what you want to do?'

'Yes I am. I like Twynham very much but
there's no place like home. Besides, I can come
back here for holidays and stay at a nice hotel.
You can come too. I shall be able to afford
that.' She went to the window and with her
back to him said, 'I thought at first I'd make
the cottage over to Danny. Then I thought, if
Edith had wanted him to have it she would
have left it to him instead of me. But there was
nothing to stop me selling the cottage and
giving him some of the money.'

'That would have been very foolish.'

'I see it now but I thought he was such a nice
boy. I only wanted to help him. That's why I
didn't want you to tell the police about him. I
wanted him to have a second chance.'

'He's had plenty of those,' thought Bits and Pieces but he did not say so.

A week later they returned home to the unbounded joy of Barney who had greatly missed his master. His brothers too were glad to see him. 'Not that there's much for you to take to market. Nobody's giving anything away,' John said.

'Wait 'til the van arrives from Cockleshell Cottage. Mrs G. has given me a load of stuff; nice, interesting bits that'll fetch good prices – pictures, ornaments, china, books, heaps of things. Business will perk up no end. You'll see.'

When all the talking was over and the junk yard closed he took Barney for a walk down Dwelly Lane where he had first met Artemisia the witch. Bluebells and primroses peeped through the hedgerows and everywhere trees and bushes wore a green tinge.

Presently he leant on a gate and stared across a rolling meadow to the gentle hills beyond. In his mind's eye he was back in Twynham where monks had once ground their corn and smugglers plied their illicit trade; where prehistoric man had dwelt and local chieftains were buried over a thousand years ago; where a busy river throbbed with life and men and boys fished to their heart's content and he knew he would take *his* fishing rod the next time he went there.

A woman came through the trees. She was neither young nor old, short nor tall, but when she smiled he knew she was Artemisia. Excitedly, he ran to meet her and the mop flew out of his pocket and buried itself in her gown.

'Are you taking it back? Have I lost Moppy?' he asked.

'How can I take back something I gave willingly? Did I not promise that the mop would be a good friend to you?'

'You did and it is. Moppy's the best friend I ever had.'

'Then keep it safely for who knows how soon you will have need of it again.'

At her words the magic mop flew back into the junk man's pocket and Artemisia was gone. Bits and Pieces felt Barney's warm tongue on his hand and stroked the dog's head.

'I should have said *one* of my two best friends for of course Barney you are the other . . .'